I0018722

"Samsung Galaxy S25 Ultra: A Buyer's Guide"

CHARLES WRIGHT

All rights reserved. No part of this publication may be reproduced, distributed, or transmitted in any form or by any means, including photocopying, recording, or other electronic or mechanical methods, without the prior written permission of the publisher, except in the case of brief quotations embodied in critical reviews and certain other noncommercial uses permitted by copyright law.

Charles Wright. © 2025

Table of contents

Chapter 1:

Introduction

1.1 Overview of the Samsung Galaxy S25 Ultra

Overview of the Samsung Galaxy S25 Ultra The Samsung Galaxy S25 Ultra is the pinnacle of smartphone innovation, representing the latest advancements in mobile technology. As the flagship device for 2025, it combines cutting-edge hardware, intelligent software, and refined design to deliver an unparalleled user experience. Whether you're a professional looking for productivity tools, a photography enthusiast, or someone seeking top-tier performance, the Galaxy S25 Ultra caters to all. Equipped with a massive 6.8-inch Dynamic AMOLED 2X display, the device offers vibrant visuals, sharp clarity, and adaptive refresh rates of up to 144Hz for smooth scrolling and gaming. Powered by the Snapdragon 8 Gen 4 processor, it ensures lightning-fast performance and energy efficiency, making it ideal for multitasking and resource-intensive tasks. With configurations offering up to 16GB of RAM and 1TB of storage, users have plenty of space for apps, files, and media. The camera system is one of its standout features. The quad-camera setup includes a 200MP primary sensor, which captures stunning detail, even in challenging lighting conditions. Additionally, advanced video recording capabilities such as 8K resolution at 60fps make it a top choice for content creators. Paired with AI-powered enhancements, the phone ensures that every photo and video meets professional standards. Battery life and charging technology also receive significant upgrades. With a 5,500mAh battery, users can expect all-day performance, while 100W wired and 50W wireless charging capabilities mean less downtime. New features like satellite connectivity provide reliable communication in remote areas, ensuring that the Galaxy S25 Ultra goes beyond traditional smartphone functionality. The Galaxy S25 Ultra runs on Android 15 with Samsung's One UI 7.1, offering a seamless and intuitive interface. Samsung's commitment to long-term software support—up to seven years of updates—makes it a future-proof choice for those looking to invest in a durable and reliable smartphone.

1.2 The Legacy of Samsung's Flagship Series

Samsung's flagship Galaxy series has been synonymous with innovation and excellence in the smartphone market. Since the launch of the original Galaxy S in 2010, the series has consistently raised the bar for what smartphones can achieve. Each iteration has introduced groundbreaking features, setting trends and pushing the boundaries of technology. The Galaxy S series is renowned for its focus on premium design, cutting-edge hardware, and user-centric software. Over the years, Samsung has pioneered technologies like Super AMOLED displays, high-resolution cameras, and advanced multitasking capabilities. The introduction of the Galaxy Note's S Pen functionality into the Ultra models further cemented Samsung's reputation as a leader in productivity-focused devices. Samsung has also been at the forefront of mobile photography. From introducing optical image stabilization to incorporating high-resolution sensors, the company has consistently delivered some of the best smartphone cameras in the industry. The Galaxy S Ultra models, in particular, have become a favorite for those seeking professional-grade photography and videography tools in a pocket-sized device. In addition to hardware innovation, Samsung's software ecosystem has evolved to provide a more integrated experience. Features like Samsung DeX, which turns your phone into a desktop computer, and SmartThings, which connects various devices in a smart home, have highlighted the versatility of the Galaxy series. Samsung has also been a pioneer in software support, offering extended updates to ensure that their devices remain relevant and secure for years. The Galaxy S25 Ultra represents the culmination of this legacy, embodying the values of innovation, reliability, and user satisfaction that have defined Samsung's flagship series for over a decade. It builds on past successes while introducing forward-thinking features that position it as a smartphone for the future. For those familiar with the series, the S25 Ultra is a natural progression, offering enhancements in design, performance, and functionality. For newcomers, it's a gateway into one of the most celebrated smartphone lineups in history. The Galaxy S series isn't just a product line—it's a testament to Samsung's commitment to pushing the boundaries of technology and delivering value to its users worldwide.

Chapter 2:

Why Choose the Samsung Galaxy S25 Ultra?

2.1 What Sets It Apart from Other Smartphones

Samsung's Galaxy S25 Ultra distinguishes itself from the competition in several key ways:

1. Stunning Design and Display Technology

The Galaxy S25 Ultra boasts a 6.8-inch Dynamic AMOLED 2X display, offering vibrant colors, deep contrasts, and exceptional clarity. Its adaptive refresh rate, which can scale up to 144Hz, ensures smooth scrolling, responsive gaming, and fluid animations. Unlike many competitors, the S25 Ultra maintains top-tier display performance without compromising battery life, thanks to its energy-efficient technology. The design is equally impressive. With a sleek and ergonomic build, the phone is comfortable to hold and exudes a premium feel. The durable materials and an IP68 water and dust resistance rating ensure the device can withstand daily wear and tear.

2. Exceptional Camera System

Photography enthusiasts will appreciate the Galaxy S25 Ultra's advanced quad-camera setup. Its 200MP primary sensor captures stunning detail and clarity, even in low-light conditions. Complemented by a 50MP ultra-wide lens, a 10MP telephoto lens with 3x optical zoom, and a 50MP periscope telephoto lens with 5x optical zoom, the phone offers versatility for capturing everything from expansive landscapes to intricate close-ups. The video capabilities are equally impressive, with support for 8K recording at 60fps, ensuring high-resolution videos with smooth motion. AI enhancements and features like Super Steady mode make it easy to capture professional-quality footage.

3. Unparalleled Performance At its core

the Galaxy S25 Ultra is powered by the Snapdragon 8 Gen 4 processor, which delivers lightning-fast performance and efficient power management. Whether you're gaming, multitasking, or editing videos, the device handles everything with ease. Paired with up to 16GB of RAM and storage options up to 1TB, it provides ample space and speed for demanding tasks.

4. Extended Software Support

One of the standout features of the Galaxy S25 Ultra is Samsung's commitment to long-term software updates. With up to seven years of

Android OS and security updates, users can enjoy the latest features and protections without needing to upgrade their device frequently.

5. Satellite Connectivity

In a move that sets it apart from many competitors, the S25 Ultra includes satellite connectivity. This feature allows users to stay connected in remote areas without cellular coverage, making it an excellent choice for adventurers and travelers.

2.2 Key Advantages of Owning the S25 Ultra

1. Productivity on the Go

The Galaxy S25 Ultra is designed for those who need to stay productive. With features like Samsung DeX, users can transform their phone into a desktop-like experience, connecting it to a monitor, keyboard, and mouse. The large screen and powerful processor make multitasking seamless, whether you're working on documents, attending virtual meetings, or managing emails.

2. Superior Entertainment Experience

The device offers an immersive entertainment experience, thanks to its superior display and audio capabilities. The high refresh rate, combined with HDR10+ support, makes watching videos and playing games a delight. Stereo speakers tuned by AKG ensure rich and clear audio, enhancing your overall media consumption.

3. Long Battery Life and Fast Charging

With a 5,500mAh battery, the Galaxy S25 Ultra provides all-day performance, even for heavy users. Its 100W wired and 50W wireless fast charging capabilities ensure that you can quickly recharge and get back to using your device without long interruptions. Reverse wireless charging is another useful feature, allowing you to power other devices on the go.

4. Future-Proof Investment

The combination of cutting-edge hardware, long-term software support, and durable build quality makes the Galaxy S25 Ultra a future-proof investment. It's a phone designed to remain relevant and reliable for years, offering excellent value for its premium price.

5. Advanced Security and Privacy Features

Samsung continues to prioritize user security, and the S25 Ultra is no exception. The device features an ultrasonic fingerprint scanner for secure and fast unlocking. Samsung Knox, the company's proprietary security platform, provides additional layers of protection for sensitive data. Features like Secure Folder and Private Share ensure that your personal and professional information remains safe.

6. A Versatile Camera for Every Situation

Whether you're capturing memories with friends, shooting professional-grade photos, or experimenting with creative photography, the S25 Ultra's camera system delivers. Its AI-powered scene optimization and pro-grade editing tools make it a versatile choice for photographers of all levels.

7. Ecosystem Integration

The Galaxy S25 Ultra seamlessly integrates with Samsung's ecosystem of devices and services. From pairing with Galaxy Buds for superior audio quality to syncing with Galaxy Watches for health tracking and notifications, the device enhances your connected lifestyle. Samsung SmartThings adds another layer of convenience, allowing you to control smart home devices directly from your phone.

Chapter 3:

Design and Display

3.1 Premium Build and Ergonomic Design

When you hold the Galaxy S25 Ultra, it's clear that it's crafted with attention to detail and premium materials. The sleek, modern design combines an aluminum frame with a glass back, giving the phone a sophisticated feel that is both durable and stylish. The combination of materials ensures that the device remains lightweight while providing a robust, high-end finish.

The phone's dimensions are carefully balanced to offer a large screen while maintaining comfortable handling. Despite its sizable 6.8-inch display, the S25 Ultra's slim profile and rounded edges make it easy to hold in one hand. The placement of the camera array at the back is seamlessly integrated into the phone's overall design, with the lenses encased in a clean, minimalist housing that complements the device's elegance.

Additionally, the Galaxy S25 Ultra is rated with an IP68 certification, meaning it's dust and water-resistant. This adds an extra layer of protection, ensuring that the phone can withstand accidental spills, splashes, or even brief immersion in water. Whether you're using it outdoors, at the beach, or in a rainy setting, the S25 Ultra is built to last, giving users peace of mind with its durability.

Samsung's thoughtful approach to design ensures that the Galaxy S25 Ultra not only looks great but also feels great to use. The carefully considered ergonomics of the device, such as button placements and curved edges, make it comfortable to operate even for extended periods, providing an enjoyable user experience.

3.2 Dynamic AMOLED 2X Display Features

One of the key highlights of the Galaxy S25 Ultra is its 6.8-inch Dynamic AMOLED 2X display. This display technology offers a breathtaking viewing experience with vibrant colors, deep blacks, and excellent contrast ratios. Samsung has refined this AMOLED technology over the years, and the S25 Ultra's display is a testament to the company's commitment to pushing the limits of mobile screen technology.

Dynamic AMOLED 2X provides exceptional clarity and brightness, making it ideal for various lighting conditions. Whether you're outdoors on a bright sunny day or in a dimly lit room, the display automatically adjusts to maintain visibility without straining your eyes. With a peak brightness of up to 1750 nits, the screen remains legible even under intense sunlight, ensuring that you can enjoy content wherever you are.

The display also supports HDR10+, which enhances the contrast and color accuracy of videos, providing more vibrant and lifelike visuals. For movie lovers, content streamed on platforms like Netflix or YouTube will appear more dynamic and immersive, bringing out the rich details in each scene. This is particularly noticeable when watching high-definition videos or playing graphics-intensive games.

Additionally, the S25 Ultra's Dynamic AMOLED 2X display offers higher color accuracy, meaning images on the screen look true to life. For users who value visual fidelity—whether it's for photo editing, gaming, or media consumption—the screen delivers a top-tier experience.

One of the standout features of the Dynamic AMOLED 2X is its ability to maintain lower power consumption while offering vivid visuals. Samsung has optimized this display technology to deliver excellent color quality without significantly impacting battery life, which is a critical factor for users who demand a long-lasting display experience.

3.3 Adaptive Refresh Rate: A Game-Changer

The Galaxy S25 Ultra comes equipped with an adaptive refresh rate that can scale from 1Hz to 144Hz depending on the task at hand. This dynamic adjustment is one of the standout features that truly elevates the user experience.

A standard display refreshes 60 times per second, but a higher refresh rate (like 120Hz or

144Hz) makes animations, scrolling, and gameplay look significantly smoother. In fact, the Galaxy S25 Ultra's 144Hz refresh rate offers an ultra-responsive experience, especially when playing fast-paced games or swiping through apps. The smoothness of the display can make all the difference, especially for users who value fluidity and responsiveness when interacting with their phone.

However, not all tasks require such high refresh rates, and that's where the adaptive feature comes into play. When you're reading a static page, like a document or a news article, the phone automatically drops the refresh rate to 1Hz. This lower rate helps conserve battery life by reducing power consumption when the higher refresh rate isn't needed. On the other hand, when you're watching a video or playing a game, the refresh rate ramps up to 144Hz, providing a buttery-smooth visual experience. The phone adjusts this seamlessly, so you don't have to worry about toggling settings.

This adaptive refresh rate is a game-changer in terms of battery efficiency and user experience. It helps the Galaxy S25 Ultra provide a balance between high performance and energy conservation, ensuring that users can enjoy smooth visuals without sacrificing the device's longevity throughout the day.

In addition to the refresh rate, the touch response rate is another important factor for gamers and those who use the phone for precise tasks like drawing or graphic design. The Galaxy S25 Ultra features a 240Hz touch sampling rate, which makes it highly responsive to user inputs. This ensures a quicker, more accurate reaction when interacting with the screen, whether you're tapping, scrolling, or swiping.

Chapter 4:

Performance and Hardware

4.1 Snapdragon 8 Gen 4 Processor: Unmatched Speed

At the heart of the Samsung Galaxy S25 Ultra is the Snapdragon 8 Gen 4 processor. This chipset is the latest in Qualcomm's line of high-performance processors, designed to push the boundaries of mobile performance. The Snapdragon 8 Gen 4 offers significant improvements in speed, efficiency, and power compared to its predecessors, making it one of the most powerful mobile processors available.

With its enhanced CPU and GPU architecture, the Snapdragon 8 Gen 4 ensures that everything runs smoothly, whether you're browsing the web, playing graphics-heavy games, or multitasking between several apps. Its powerful octa-core design combines high-performance cores for demanding tasks with efficient cores for lighter workloads, allowing for a perfect balance between power and battery efficiency.

One of the most noticeable benefits of the Snapdragon 8 Gen 4 is its speed. Applications load almost instantly, and multitasking is seamless. Switching between apps or working with multiple apps open at once is a breeze, thanks to the increased processing power. Whether you're editing photos, rendering videos, or working with large files, the S25 Ultra's processor handles it all without a hitch, ensuring a fast and responsive experience.

The chip's enhanced GPU performance makes the S25 Ultra an excellent choice for gaming. Mobile gaming has never been more immersive, with the Snapdragon 8 Gen 4 delivering smooth, high-quality graphics at high frame rates. Graphics-intensive games run without lag, and demanding titles look stunning, thanks to the GPU's ability to render realistic visuals and effects.

4.2 Memory and Storage Options

The Samsung Galaxy S25 Ultra is designed to handle large amounts of data and memory-intensive tasks with ease. It comes with a range of memory and storage configurations, ensuring that users can select the right setup based on their needs.

The device is available with up to 16GB of RAM, which is more than enough to handle heavy multitasking and demanding apps. Whether you're running several apps in the background, browsing with numerous tabs open, or switching between multiple programs, the ample RAM ensures that the phone runs efficiently and without lag. Even with memory-intensive apps like video editors, graphic design tools, or resource-heavy games, the S25 Ultra's 16GB of RAM provides smooth performance.

In terms of storage, the Galaxy S25 Ultra offers up to 1TB of internal storage, which is ideal for users who store large files, such as videos, photos, documents, and apps. For those who need even more storage, the phone supports microSD cards, giving users the flexibility to expand their storage capacity. The large storage options are especially useful for people who need to store high-definition videos or large photo libraries, making the device an excellent choice for content creators, professionals, and power users.

With such high amounts of RAM and storage, users can expect long-term performance that remains fast and responsive over time. The phone is designed to handle demanding tasks for years without slowing down, making it a future-proof investment for those who require the best in mobile performance.

4.3 AI Integration and User Experience

Artificial intelligence (AI) is integrated throughout the Samsung Galaxy S25 Ultra to enhance the user experience in ways that traditional smartphones cannot match. The phone uses AI in several areas, from photography to battery management, making it smarter, more intuitive, and highly responsive.

AI in Photography

The S25 Ultra's AI capabilities shine most clearly in its camera system. The phone uses AI to automatically detect scenes and optimize settings in real-time for the best possible shots. Whether you're taking a picture of a landscape, a portrait, or a low-light scene, the AI analyzes the image and adjusts the camera settings to capture the most accurate, detailed, and vibrant photo possible. This intelligent processing means you don't need to fiddle with settings to get a professional-quality shot, making photography easier for everyone—from amateurs to advanced users.

AI for Performance Optimization

The Galaxy S25 Ultra also uses AI to manage system resources more efficiently. AI algorithms monitor how you use your phone and adjust performance levels accordingly. For example, the phone might automatically adjust the refresh rate based on your usage, increase processing power for demanding apps, or throttle performance when you're engaged in less resource-heavy tasks. This dynamic performance optimization not only boosts speed and responsiveness but also improves battery life by reducing power consumption during low-intensity use.

AI in Battery Management

The S25 Ultra uses AI to optimize battery life by learning your usage patterns and adjusting the charging and power consumption accordingly. It can predict when you need more battery and when you're likely to use less, ensuring that the battery lasts as long as possible. Features like adaptive power-saving mode allow the device to intelligently manage its energy consumption, which is particularly useful for heavy users who want to make the most out of their battery throughout the day.

AI for Personalized User Experience

The Galaxy S25 Ultra's AI features extend to the software as well. The device uses machine learning to predict your habits and adjust the interface and notifications to suit your needs. For example, the phone may suggest apps you are likely to use based on your previous behavior, or it might prioritize notifications from the apps you use most. This results in a more personalized and efficient user experience, allowing you to get the most out of your device without having to manually adjust settings.

Chapter 5:

Camera Capabilities

5.1 Quad-Camera System Overview

The Galaxy S25 Ultra is equipped with a sophisticated quad-camera system designed to handle any photography situation, from ultra-wide landscapes to detailed close-ups. This versatile setup includes:

200MP Primary Camera

The centerpiece of the camera system is the 200MP primary sensor, which offers exceptional detail and clarity in every shot. This ultra-high-resolution camera captures incredible amounts of detail, making it ideal for large-scale prints or cropping images without losing sharpness. The 200MP camera also performs exceptionally well in low-light conditions, thanks to advanced sensor technology that enhances brightness and clarity even in dim environments.

50MP Ultra-Wide Camera

For those wide-angle shots or sweeping landscapes, the 50MP ultra-wide camera provides a broad perspective with minimal distortion. Whether you're photographing scenic vistas or large groups, this lens ensures that you capture everything in sharp detail, maintaining true color and crispness.

10MP Telephoto Camera (3x Optical Zoom)

The 10MP telephoto camera offers 3x optical zoom, allowing you to get closer to your subject without sacrificing image quality. This lens is perfect for portraits or any situation where you need to zoom in on a subject from a distance. The lens also features optical image stabilization (OIS), reducing motion blur and ensuring sharper, clearer images even when zoomed in.

50MP Periscope Telephoto Camera (5x Optical Zoom)

For even greater zoom, the 50MP periscope telephoto lens offers 5x optical zoom. This is ideal for capturing distant subjects without compromising detail. Whether you're shooting wildlife, architecture, or sports, this lens ensures that you can zoom in without losing clarity. The periscope design allows for a more compact zoom mechanism, enabling a longer focal length without increasing the thickness of the phone.

Together, these four lenses provide unmatched flexibility and versatility, allowing users to capture everything from ultra-wide panoramas to distant details with exceptional clarity.

5.2 Advanced Photography and Video Features

The Samsung Galaxy S25 Ultra is designed not just for everyday snapshots, but for advanced photographers and videographers who demand professional-grade results. With its advanced photography and video features, the S25 Ultra ensures that you can capture stunning imagery in any situation.

8K Video Recording

One of the most impressive features of the Galaxy S25 Ultra's camera system is its ability to record in 8K resolution at 30 frames per second. This ultra-high-definition video resolution offers a level of detail that surpasses traditional 4K and provides an incredibly immersive viewing experience. Whether you're recording an event, a special moment, or creating content for social media, 8K video ensures that every detail is captured in breathtaking clarity.

Super Steady Mode

For those moments when you're on the move, the Super Steady mode helps capture smooth, shake-free video. Whether you're walking, running, or recording from a moving vehicle, this feature compensates for camera shake and ensures that your videos stay steady. This makes it an excellent tool for action shots, travel videos, or vlogs, allowing you to record dynamic content without worrying about blurriness or uneven footage.

Director's View

Director's View is a unique feature that allows users to capture video from multiple lenses simultaneously. This feature gives videographers the ability to switch between the front and rear cameras and zoom levels, all while recording. It's perfect for those who need to capture a variety of perspectives or create dynamic videos that change angles quickly, all without pausing the recording.

Pro Mode

For photographers who want full control over their shots, the Galaxy S25 Ultra offers a Pro Mode that allows manual adjustments to settings like ISO, shutter speed, aperture, and white balance. This level of control ensures that you can achieve exactly the look you want, whether you're shooting in low light or capturing fine details in bright sunlight.

Night Mode

The Galaxy S25 Ultra excels in low-light conditions, thanks to its advanced Night Mode. This mode allows you to take clear, detailed photos in dark environments without the need for a flash. The phone's sensor gathers more light and uses AI processing to reduce noise and enhance image detail, delivering bright and sharp photos even in near-complete darkness.

8K Snap

After recording a video in 8K, the S25 Ultra offers an innovative feature called 8K Snap, which allows you to extract high-quality still photos from the video. This means that even if you're recording an action-packed video, you can later capture stunning individual frames without losing resolution, making it ideal for moments when you need to capture a specific shot from a video.

5.3 AI Enhancements for Stunning Shots

One of the standout features of the Samsung Galaxy S25 Ultra is its use of artificial intelligence (AI) to improve the quality of photos and videos. AI is integrated into the camera system in a variety of ways, making it easier for users to capture stunning images without needing to adjust settings manually.

Scene Optimization

The AI-powered scene optimizer automatically detects what you're photographing and adjusts settings accordingly. Whether you're capturing a landscape, a portrait, a food shot, or a pet, the camera intelligently enhances the colors, contrast, and brightness for the best possible result. This eliminates the guesswork, ensuring that you get professional-quality shots without needing to be a photography expert.

AI Image Processing

Samsung's AI-powered image processing helps to reduce noise and enhance details in images, particularly in low-light conditions. AI is used to improve color accuracy, sharpness, and contrast, giving your photos a more vibrant and polished look. It also works in real-time, so you can see the enhancements as you take the shot, ensuring the best result every time.

Portrait Mode

The S25 Ultra's portrait mode, which uses AI to detect faces and enhance the background blur, makes portrait photography stand out. The AI can differentiate between the subject and background, allowing it to create a professional "bokeh" effect, where the subject is sharply in focus while the background is beautifully blurred. This makes portraits appear more professional, similar to what you'd see from a DSLR camera.

Object and Scene Detection

The AI also helps to automatically detect objects and scenes, adjusting settings to ensure optimal focus, exposure, and composition. Whether you're photographing a sunset, a busy street, or a close-up of a flower, the camera's AI makes sure that the subject is highlighted and well-exposed, ensuring that your photos look natural and balanced.

AI-Enhanced Video Stabilization

In addition to photography, AI also plays a crucial role in video stabilization. Whether you're recording handheld or capturing fast-moving subjects, the Galaxy S25 Ultra uses AI to smooth out video footage, making it appear steady even in challenging conditions. This ensures that your videos stay smooth and professional-looking, no matter how dynamic the action.

Chapter 6:

Battery and Charging

6.1 Battery Life: Powering Your Day

The Samsung Galaxy S25 Ultra is equipped with a large, high-capacity battery designed to keep up with the demands of users who rely on their smartphones for everything from work to entertainment. With a 5,000mAh battery, the Galaxy S25 Ultra offers ample power to last through a busy day, even with heavy usage.

All-Day Power

The 5,000mAh battery provides enough energy to get you through a full day of use without needing to recharge. Whether you're browsing the internet, watching videos, playing games, or using apps, the phone is capable of handling extended screen-on time. With moderate use, users can expect the phone to last from morning until night, depending on individual usage habits. Even for power users who engage in resource-intensive tasks, the Galaxy S25 Ultra's battery is engineered to keep pace with the demands of the day.

Efficient Power Management

One of the key factors contributing to the Galaxy S25 Ultra's impressive battery life is its advanced power management features. The phone's software intelligently manages power consumption, adjusting settings and performance based on your usage patterns. For example, when you're using less demanding apps or tasks, the phone may lower the screen brightness or reduce background activity to preserve battery life. Additionally, the adaptive refresh rate, which automatically adjusts the screen's refresh rate based on the task at hand, helps minimize power usage when high refresh rates are not necessary. This dynamic management ensures that the phone consumes energy efficiently, allowing it to last longer without compromising on performance.

The device also benefits from AI-driven battery optimization, which learns your usage habits over time. This allows the phone to make smarter decisions about which apps to keep active and how to conserve power, ensuring that your battery lasts longer when you need it most.

Power Saving Modes

For users who need extra longevity, the Galaxy S25 Ultra offers power-saving modes that can extend battery life. These modes limit background activities, reduce screen brightness, and adjust other settings to ensure the battery lasts longer in critical situations. Whether you're on the go and away from a charger for a while, or you simply want to stretch out the battery during a long workday, these modes provide a convenient way to maximize battery life without sacrificing core functionality.

6.2 Fast Charging and Wireless Charging Technology

The Samsung Galaxy S25 Ultra doesn't just focus on battery life—it also excels in charging technology, offering both fast wired and wireless charging solutions to ensure that users spend less time plugged in and more time on the move. Here's a closer look at the charging capabilities:

Fast Charging

The Galaxy S25 Ultra supports 45W fast charging, which is one of the fastest charging speeds available on any smartphone. With this high-speed charging technology, the S25 Ultra can go from 0% to 50% in just 20-30 minutes, making it incredibly convenient for users who need to quickly top up their battery during a busy day. In about an hour, you can expect the phone to be fully charged, allowing you to get back to using your device with minimal downtime.

This rapid charging capability is perfect for those times when you need to get a quick charge before heading out or when you're in a rush. Thanks to its efficient charging system, the Galaxy S25 Ultra ensures that you can power up in a flash without waiting long periods for a full charge.

Wireless Charging

For users who prefer the convenience of charging without the need for cables, the Galaxy S25 Ultra supports wireless charging at speeds of up to 15W. This allows you to simply place the phone on a wireless charging pad and let it charge without having to plug in any cables. Whether at home, at the office, or in public spaces with available wireless charging stations, the S25 Ultra offers a seamless charging experience.

The wireless charging feature is especially useful when you want to charge your phone overnight or while multitasking, as you don't have to worry about plugging and unplugging cables. Additionally, the phone is compatible with Samsung's Fast Wireless Charging 2.0 technology, ensuring that it charges quickly and efficiently even without a wired connection.

Reverse Wireless Charging

In addition to regular wireless charging, the Galaxy S25 Ultra also supports reverse wireless charging. This innovative feature allows the phone to wirelessly charge other devices, such as headphones, smartwatches, or even other smartphones. Simply place the device on the back of the Galaxy S25 Ultra, and it will start charging. This feature is especially useful when you're traveling or on the go, allowing you to charge your accessories without needing to carry extra cables or power banks.

Battery Health and Longevity

Samsung has incorporated advanced charging management features that help preserve the health and longevity of the battery. These features include optimized charging practices, such as reducing the charge speed when the battery is near full, helping to prevent overcharging and minimize heat buildup. The phone also includes a battery care function that monitors the charge cycle to ensure that the battery maintains optimal health over time.

Chapter 7:

Software and Features

7.1 Android 15 and One UI 7.1: A Perfect Pair

The Galaxy S25 Ultra runs on Android 15, the latest iteration of Google's mobile operating system. Android 15 brings several enhancements, focusing on performance, security, and user experience. It offers smoother animations, better app management, and increased customization options, allowing users to tailor their smartphones to suit their personal preferences.

However, what truly sets the Galaxy S25 Ultra apart is One UI 7.1, Samsung's custom user interface that sits on top of Android. One UI has evolved over the years to become one of the most user-friendly and feature-rich interfaces available on Android devices. One UI 7.1 adds several improvements, making the Galaxy S25 Ultra even more intuitive and customizable.

User-Friendly Interface

One of the standout features of One UI is its focus on one-handed use. The interface is designed to place essential features within easy reach, particularly on larger devices like the S25 Ultra. With One UI 7.1, Samsung continues to refine this approach, making it even easier to navigate the large 6.8-inch display without straining your hand.

Enhanced Customization

One UI 7.1 allows users to personalize the device to their liking. You can choose from a wide range of themes, icons, and wallpapers to make the device feel uniquely yours. Additionally, with a host of widgets and quick toggles, you can adjust settings and access apps without having to dive deep into the menus. The customizability extends to the lock screen, home screen, and even the Always-On Display, ensuring that every user can make the phone their own.

Improved Multitasking

One UI 7.1 further enhances multitasking capabilities. The feature-rich multi-window mode makes it easy to run two apps side by side or use pop-up windows for more fluid multitasking. Whether you're browsing the web while responding to emails or watching a video while taking notes, the S25 Ultra's multitasking features allow you to seamlessly switch between tasks and boost your productivity.

Security and Privacy Enhancements

In addition to the usual performance improvements, One UI 7.1 also includes several security and privacy features designed to keep your data safe. One UI integrates biometric authentication options like the ultrasonic fingerprint scanner and facial recognition, both of which are fast, accurate, and secure. Samsung also includes a Privacy Dashboard that allows users to easily track how apps are using their data and location, offering a transparent approach to privacy management.

7.2 Satellite Connectivity: A New Frontier

The Samsung Galaxy S25 Ultra introduces satellite connectivity, a groundbreaking feature that sets it apart from most smartphones currently on the market. Satellite connectivity allows users to send and receive messages even when there is no cellular signal available, by tapping into satellite networks in areas where traditional mobile networks are out of reach.

Emergency Communication in Remote Areas

One of the most practical uses of satellite connectivity is emergency communication in remote or rural areas, where cellular networks may not be available. The S25 Ultra's satellite connectivity allows you to send emergency messages, including your GPS location, when you're stranded or in danger. This feature could prove invaluable for hikers, travelers, and outdoor enthusiasts who often find themselves in locations without mobile coverage.

Reliable, Global Coverage

Satellite connectivity also enables global coverage, meaning you can stay connected even when you're traveling in remote parts of the world. Whether you're on a hiking trip in the mountains or sailing in the middle of the ocean, the ability to stay connected via satellite ensures that you're always in touch, whether for safety or for convenience.

Seamless Integration

Samsung has ensured that satellite connectivity works seamlessly within the existing messaging app. Users don't need to install any third-party apps or make complicated settings adjustments. Simply open the messaging app, and if a satellite connection is available, you'll see an option to send a message via satellite. The user interface is designed to make this process as smooth as possible, ensuring that even in emergency situations, users can easily send messages and access help.

7.3 Extended Software Support for Longevity

One of the critical factors that determine the longevity of a smartphone is the length of time it will receive software updates. Samsung has taken significant steps to address this issue with the Galaxy S25 Ultra, offering extended software support to ensure that the device stays up-to-date with the latest features and security patches over time.

Three Years of Major Updates

The Galaxy S25 Ultra will receive three years of major software updates, ensuring that it gets the latest Android features, enhancements, and optimizations. This means that users won't be left behind after a few years of use, as they will continue to receive the latest Android features and improvements, much like when the phone was first launched.

Four Years of Security Updates

In addition to major software updates, the Galaxy S25 Ultra also comes with four years of security updates. These regular security patches help protect the device from vulnerabilities and threats that may emerge over time. With the rapid pace of technological advancement and the increasing focus on cybersecurity, having access to these updates is crucial to keeping your device safe and secure.

Optimized Performance Over Time

Samsung's extended software support also contributes to the device's long-term performance. Through periodic software updates, the phone's operating system is optimized to ensure smooth operation even as apps and features evolve. Users can expect their Galaxy S25 Ultra to maintain a high level of performance throughout its lifespan, with fewer slowdowns or issues that might typically arise as the device ages.

One UI Updates

In addition to Android updates, Samsung's One UI will also receive regular updates to enhance the overall user experience. New features, design changes, and improvements are often included in One UI updates, ensuring that users continue to have access to the best possible version of the software. With Samsung's commitment to software excellence, the Galaxy S25 Ultra is designed to remain a reliable and high-performing device for years to come.

Chapter 8

Who Should Buy the Samsung Galaxy S25 Ultra?

8.1 Ideal Users and Use Cases

The Samsung Galaxy S25 Ultra is designed for users who seek top-tier performance, innovative features, and the best of what modern smartphones can offer. Whether you're a professional, a tech enthusiast, or someone who simply enjoys the latest in mobile technology, the Galaxy S25 Ultra is built to meet diverse needs. Here are some of the ideal users for this smartphone:

1. Power Users and Multitaskers

For those who juggle multiple tasks throughout the day and require a phone that can keep up, the Galaxy S25 Ultra is an ideal choice. With its powerful Snapdragon 8 Gen 4 processor, large RAM options, and smooth multitasking capabilities, the S25 Ultra can easily handle demanding tasks like video editing, gaming, and running several apps simultaneously. Its One UI 7.1 interface further enhances multitasking by allowing users to split their screen, use pop-up windows, and quickly switch between tasks. Power users who need reliability and performance will appreciate the S25 Ultra's ability to handle everything without slowing down.

2. Professional Photographers and Content Creators

The quad-camera system and advanced photography features on the Galaxy S25 Ultra make it an excellent option for professional photographers and content creators. Whether you're capturing detailed landscapes, creating high-quality videos, or snapping portraits, the phone's powerful camera system, including its 108MP wide sensor and 10x optical zoom, ensures that you'll have the tools necessary for stunning shots in any situation. Content creators will benefit from features like 8K video recording and enhanced AI processing that helps produce professional-grade content on the go, without the need for additional equipment.

3. Tech Enthusiasts and Early Adopters

The Galaxy S25 Ultra is packed with cutting-edge features that make it an attractive choice for tech enthusiasts and early adopters who enjoy having the latest and greatest technology at their fingertips. With satellite connectivity, which enables communication even in areas without a cellular signal, and 5G compatibility, the S25 Ultra is ahead of the curve in terms of both connectivity and innovation. The Dynamic AMOLED 2X display, coupled with the adaptive refresh rate, offers a top-tier visual experience that appeals to those who demand high-quality screens for gaming, media consumption, or productivity.

4. Frequent Travelers and Outdoor Enthusiasts

For individuals who travel frequently or spend a lot of time outdoors, the Samsung Galaxy S25 Ultra is a perfect companion. Satellite connectivity ensures that users can send emergency messages and maintain communication even in remote areas where traditional mobile networks are unavailable. Its 5,000mAh battery offers impressive battery life, so users don't have to worry about running out of power during long days of travel. The durable design, coupled with IP68 water and dust resistance, means the S25 Ultra can withstand various weather conditions, making it a reliable device for those who are often on the go.

5. Business Professionals and Productivity Seekers

Business professionals who require a device that can handle both work and personal life will find the Galaxy S25 Ultra a suitable choice. With its high performance, long battery life, and multitasking capabilities, it can easily support work-related tasks such as video conferencing, document editing, and project management. Features like Samsung Dex allow users to turn their phone into a desktop-like experience by connecting to a monitor, making it a great tool for professionals who need to be productive even when they're away from a traditional workspace.

6. Mobile Gamers

For mobile gaming enthusiasts, the Samsung Galaxy S25 Ultra offers a premium gaming experience. Powered by the Snapdragon 8 Gen 4 chipset, the phone can handle even the most demanding mobile games with ease. The large Dynamic AMOLED 2X display with a high refresh rate provides an immersive visual experience, while the adaptive refresh rate ensures smooth gameplay without unnecessary power consumption. The large battery ensures that gaming sessions are not interrupted by low power, making the S25 Ultra a top choice for gamers.

8.2 Tailored Features for Specific Needs

The Samsung Galaxy S25 Ultra is equipped with a variety of features that cater to the specific needs of different users. Here are some of the standout features designed for specific use cases:

1. Satellite Connectivity for Remote Communication

For frequent travelers or outdoor adventurers, satellite connectivity is a game-changer. This feature allows users to stay connected, even in places without cellular service, by sending messages via satellite. Whether you're hiking in the mountains or traveling to a remote location, the ability to send emergency messages and share your location is invaluable. The Satellite Connectivity feature is tailored to those who often find themselves in areas where traditional communication networks are unreliable or unavailable.

2. Advanced Camera System for Professional Photography

The Galaxy S25 Ultra's camera system is specifically tailored for those who require top-tier photography capabilities. The 108MP wide sensor, paired with the 12MP ultra-wide sensor, 10MP periscope telephoto lens, and 10MP telephoto lens, makes it perfect for capturing high-resolution photos and videos in any setting. Whether you're a professional photographer or a hobbyist, the camera system is designed to deliver stunning results.

Features like 8K video recording and AI-enhanced photography ensure that your photos and videos are crisp, clear, and full of detail.

3. Performance Features for Power Users

Power users and multitaskers will find the Snapdragon 8 Gen 4 processor, paired with up to 16GB of RAM, ideal for handling resource-intensive tasks. Whether you're running multiple apps, editing videos, or playing high-performance games, the S25 Ultra is built to deliver. The One UI 7.1 interface also enhances the experience by offering intuitive multitasking tools like split-screen mode, pop-up windows, and more.

4. Battery Features for Long Days

With its 5,000mAh battery, the Galaxy S25 Ultra is designed for users who need their phone to last all day without constantly worrying about charging. Whether you're on a business trip, exploring a new city, or spending the day outdoors, the phone's battery life ensures that you can stay connected, productive, and entertained without interruptions. Additionally, the 45W fast charging ensures that when you do need to charge, you can power up quickly.

5. Productivity Features for Business Users

For business professionals, the Galaxy S25 Ultra offers a variety of features aimed at improving productivity. Samsung DeX allows users to transform their phone into a desktop-like experience when connected to a monitor, enabling users to handle tasks like word processing, spreadsheet editing, and presentations with ease. The multitasking capabilities and large screen make it easy to switch between apps and stay productive throughout the day.

Chapter 9

Comparison with Competitors

9.1 Head-to-Head with iPhone 16 Pro Max

The iPhone 16 Pro Max is Apple's flagship device, offering exceptional performance, an advanced camera system, and a premium design. Let's compare the two smartphones across several key aspects:

Performance and Processor

The Galaxy S25 Ultra is powered by the Snapdragon 8 Gen 4 processor, while the iPhone 16 Pro Max features Apple's A17 Bionic chip. Both processors are highly capable, but

Apple's A17 Bionic chip has historically led in terms of single-core performance, offering blazing-fast speeds for everyday tasks and heavy-duty applications. However, the Snapdragon 8 Gen 4 is more than sufficient to handle demanding tasks, and it supports superior GPU performance, making it an excellent choice for gaming and high-performance apps.

Camera System

Both phones boast exceptional camera setups, but Samsung's quad-camera system offers a significant edge in terms of versatility. The 108MP primary sensor of the Galaxy S25 Ultra allows for incredibly detailed photos, and its 10x optical zoom is a standout feature, offering superior zoom capabilities compared to the iPhone 16 Pro Max's 5x optical zoom. Additionally, the Galaxy S25 Ultra supports 8K video recording, which is an industry-leading feature not yet available on the iPhone.

However, the iPhone 16 Pro Max tends to excel in color accuracy and image processing thanks to Apple's software optimizations. While the Galaxy S25 Ultra offers more advanced features in terms of camera specifications, the iPhone has historically produced more natural-looking photos in some situations, particularly in low light.

Battery and Charging

The Galaxy S25 Ultra features a 5,000mAh battery, while the iPhone 16 Pro Max comes with a slightly smaller 4,500mAh battery. While both devices provide excellent battery life, the S25 Ultra's larger battery is a key advantage, especially for heavy users. Additionally, the S25 Ultra supports 45W fast charging, allowing for much faster charging speeds compared to the iPhone 16 Pro Max's 20W charging.

The S25 Ultra also supports wireless charging and reverse wireless charging, which is useful for charging accessories like wireless earbuds or another phone. The iPhone, in contrast, offers wireless charging but lacks reverse charging capabilities.

Display Quality

Both smartphones feature stunning displays, but the Galaxy S25 Ultra's Dynamic AMOLED 2X display has an edge in terms of brightness, color vibrancy, and refresh rate. The S25 Ultra supports an adaptive refresh rate of up to 120Hz, while the iPhone 16 Pro Max has a ProMotion display that also supports 120Hz but lacks the same dynamic adjustment that the Galaxy offers to save battery life.

In terms of screen size, the S25 Ultra's 6.8-inch display provides a larger viewing area compared to the iPhone 16 Pro Max's 6.7-inch screen, which can make a noticeable difference for media consumption and gaming.

Software and Ecosystem

One of the key distinctions between the Galaxy S25 Ultra and iPhone 16 Pro Max is the operating system. The S25 Ultra runs on Android 15 with One UI 7.1, which offers extensive customization options and flexibility. On the other hand, the iPhone 16 Pro Max runs on iOS 17, known for its smooth integration within the Apple ecosystem, offering seamless communication between devices like Macs, iPads, and Apple Watches.

For users invested in the Apple ecosystem, the iPhone 16 Pro Max might be the preferred option, while Android enthusiasts will find the Galaxy S25 Ultra more flexible and customizable.

9.2 Comparing with Google Pixel 9 Pro

The Google Pixel 9 Pro is another competitor in the premium smartphone market, known for its clean Android experience and excellent camera capabilities. Let's examine how it compares to the Galaxy S25 Ultra:

Camera Capabilities

Google's Pixel 9 Pro is renowned for its software-driven camera performance, particularly its ability to capture stunning photos in low-light conditions. While the Galaxy S25 Ultra excels in hardware with its 108MP primary sensor, 12MP ultra-wide lens, and two telephoto lenses offering 10x optical zoom, the Pixel 9 Pro focuses on computational photography with features like Night Sight and Super Res Zoom.

The Galaxy S25 Ultra, with its advanced camera array, provides more versatility, especially when it comes to zoom capabilities and 8K video recording. However, the Pixel 9 Pro might appeal more to users who prioritize software-driven photography, particularly in situations where natural lighting and real-time image processing are critical.

Display Quality

Both phones feature fantastic displays, with the Pixel 9 Pro sporting a 6.7-inch OLED display, while the Galaxy S25 Ultra boasts a larger 6.8-inch Dynamic AMOLED 2X screen. While both phones have impressive color reproduction and sharpness, the S25 Ultra's adaptive refresh rate up to 120Hz offers a smoother user experience compared to the Pixel's fixed 120Hz display.

The Galaxy S25 Ultra's Dynamic AMOLED 2X display also tends to be brighter and more vivid, offering better outdoor visibility and higher peak brightness levels, which gives it an advantage for media consumption.

Performance

Both devices feature top-tier processors, with the Pixel 9 Pro powered by Google's custom Tensor G3 chip and the S25 Ultra running on the Snapdragon 8 Gen 4. While the Tensor G3 is optimized for machine learning and AI tasks, particularly for photography and Google Assistant features, the Snapdragon 8 Gen 4 offers an all-around high-performance experience, especially for gaming and general processing power.

For users focused on raw performance, the S25 Ultra may be the better option, while the Pixel 9 Pro offers superior AI-driven tasks and a smoother Android experience thanks to Google's direct involvement in software development.

Battery Life and Charging

Both phones feature large batteries designed to last through a full day of heavy use. However, the S25 Ultra's 5,000mAh battery paired with 45W fast charging gives it a clear advantage in terms of charging speed over the Pixel 9 Pro, which supports 30W fast charging. For users who prioritize fast charging, the Galaxy S25 Ultra is the better choice.

9.3 Unique Selling Points of the S25 Ultra

While the Galaxy S25 Ultra competes head-to-head with top competitors like the iPhone 16 Pro Max and Google Pixel 9 Pro, it offers several unique features that make it a standout device:

1. Satellite Connectivity

The ability to send messages via satellite in areas with no cellular coverage is a groundbreaking feature, especially for adventurers, travelers, and anyone who spends time in remote areas. This technology offers a level of reliability and connectivity that is unmatched by the iPhone and Pixel devices.

2. 108MP Camera with 10x Optical Zoom

The quad-camera system on the Galaxy S25 Ultra, particularly its 108MP sensor and 10x optical zoom, provides unmatched photography capabilities. This level of zoom is not available on either the iPhone or the Pixel, making the S25 Ultra the go-to choice for users who need high-quality zoom shots and versatile photography.

3. Adaptive Refresh Rate

The Galaxy S25 Ultra's adaptive refresh rate up to 120Hz provides a smoother and more responsive user experience, especially when gaming or scrolling through content. It adjusts based on what you're doing, helping to conserve battery life without sacrificing performance.

4. Performance and Gaming Excellence

With the Snapdragon 8 Gen 4 and up to 16GB of RAM, the S25 Ultra is optimized for high-performance tasks like gaming, multitasking, and content creation. The combination of hardware and software makes it one of the best smartphones for users who need power, speed, and seamless performance.

Chapter 10

Pricing and Value

10.1 Justifying the Premium Price

1. Cutting-Edge Technology and Innovation

The Samsung Galaxy S25 Ultra is packed with the latest technology, which significantly contributes to its premium price. It features the Snapdragon 8 Gen 4 processor, one of the most powerful chipsets available, ensuring that the phone can handle the most demanding tasks with ease. Whether it's gaming, multitasking, or heavy-duty applications, this chipset delivers outstanding performance, providing a smooth and lag-free experience.

Another standout feature is its quad-camera system. The 108MP wide sensor and 10x optical zoom are part of the most advanced camera setup available on any smartphone. The ability to capture highly detailed images with such an impressive zoom range is a feature that many users are willing to pay a premium for. Additionally, 8K video recording, AI enhancements, and advanced photography capabilities make it an appealing choice for professionals and content creators.

2. Premium Build Quality and Display

The S25 Ultra doesn't just impress with its internal hardware, but also with its physical design. The Dynamic AMOLED 2X display offers vibrant colors, deep blacks, and an ultra-smooth 120Hz refresh rate that rivals the best screens on the market. The 6.8-inch display is large and immersive, making it perfect for media consumption, gaming, and productivity tasks. Coupled with its IP68 water and dust resistance and robust materials, the device is built to last and withstand the elements.

The phone's premium build is another reason behind its higher price. The use of high-end materials like glass and aluminum not only gives it an elegant look and feel but also contributes to its overall durability. The level of craftsmanship involved in producing such a device is reflected in the cost.

3. Long-Lasting Battery and Fast Charging

With a 5,000mAh battery, the Galaxy S25 Ultra ensures that users can go through their day without constantly worrying about running out of power. Whether you're working, gaming, or using the phone for media consumption, the battery life is more than sufficient. The added benefit of 45W fast charging allows users to quickly recharge the phone in just a short time, minimizing downtime.

For users who need a phone that can handle long days of heavy use, the S25 Ultra delivers not only with its battery capacity but also with the speed of recharging. This level of convenience and performance adds to the phone's value proposition, justifying its higher cost.

4. Advanced Features for Niche Users

The Galaxy S25 Ultra includes some features that cater to specific user groups, making it a great choice for people with unique needs. One of the most notable features is satellite connectivity, which allows users to send messages and access certain features even in remote areas without a cellular signal. This makes the device a great option for outdoor enthusiasts, travelers, and anyone who spends time in places with limited or no network coverage.

Additionally, the AI integration in the camera system and other features of the phone enhances the user experience, offering advanced editing options and real-time processing that rival professional tools. The ability to utilize advanced technologies like 5G, Wi-Fi 6, and Bluetooth 5.2 also ensures the phone remains future-proof, supporting new features and networks for years to come.

10.2 Is It Worth the Investment?

Now that we've examined the reasons behind the Samsung Galaxy S25 Ultra's premium price, the next question is whether the phone is worth the investment. The answer depends largely on individual needs and preferences, but there are several factors to consider when evaluating the overall value:

1. Value for Photography Enthusiasts and Content Creators

For photography enthusiasts and content creators, the S25 Ultra provides exceptional value. Its 108MP primary camera, combined with a versatile quad-camera system, makes it one of the most powerful smartphones for capturing high-quality images and videos. If you're someone who requires professional-grade camera capabilities but prefers the convenience of having everything in one device, the S25 Ultra delivers remarkable results, often eliminating the need for additional equipment.

Moreover, its ability to shoot 8K video and AI-enhanced photography makes it highly appealing to those who create and share visual content regularly. For these users, the device's price is justified by the quality and performance of the camera system, which can help elevate their work.

2. Value for Power Users and Multitaskers

If you are a power user who needs top-notch performance, whether for gaming, multitasking, or running resource-heavy applications, the Galaxy S25 Ultra is a solid investment. With its Snapdragon 8 Gen 4 processor and up to 16GB of RAM, it offers unrivaled speed and reliability. Whether you're switching between apps, running complex simulations, or playing the latest mobile games, the phone can handle it all without breaking a sweat.

For professionals and business users who rely on their phone for work, the Galaxy S25 Ultra offers excellent multitasking features, including the ability to run multiple apps simultaneously, use Samsung DeX for a desktop-like experience, and take advantage of 5G speeds for seamless connectivity. For users who need a phone to support their productivity needs throughout the day, the S25 Ultra is a worthy investment.

3. Value for Travelers and Outdoor Enthusiasts

For people who frequently travel or spend time outdoors, the Galaxy S25 Ultra's satellite connectivity and long-lasting battery are features that make it a valuable tool. The ability to communicate in areas with no cellular signal can be a lifesaver in emergencies, and the long battery life ensures that users stay connected and powered throughout their journey. When combined with the phone's rugged, IP68 water and dust resistance, the S25 Ultra stands out as a great option for outdoor adventurers and frequent travelers who need a reliable device in extreme conditions.

4. Comparing to Other Flagships

When comparing the Galaxy S25 Ultra to other flagship devices, such as the iPhone 16 Pro Max and the Google Pixel 9 Pro, its price is competitive given the range of features it offers. While the iPhone might excel in certain areas, such as iOS integration and certain camera processing, the S25 Ultra offers superior zoom capabilities, 8K video recording, and adaptive display technology. Additionally, it supports more customization options and features like reverse wireless charging, making it a more flexible choice for users who value versatility.

However, the investment is less justified for users who don't need all the advanced features, such as 5G connectivity or professional-grade photography capabilities. If you're someone who prefers a more basic smartphone experience, there are plenty of other devices at a lower price point that can meet your needs.

5. Long-Term Value and Longevity

Samsung promises extended software support, with the Galaxy S25 Ultra expected to receive software updates for several years. This ensures that your investment remains future-proof and that the phone continues to perform well over time. For users looking for a long-lasting device that will remain relevant for years, the S25 Ultra provides significant long-term value.

Chapter 11

Buying Considerations

11.1 Key Factors to Evaluate Before Purchase

When deciding whether to buy the Samsung Galaxy S25 Ultra, it's essential to consider various elements, such as your specific needs, budget, and how the phone integrates with your daily life. Here are some key factors to keep in mind:

1. Performance Needs

The S25 Ultra offers top-tier performance, thanks to the Snapdragon 8 Gen 4 processor and ample RAM (up to 16GB). If you regularly engage in activities like gaming, video editing, or multitasking with multiple apps, this phone can easily meet your demands. However, if you primarily use your phone for calls, social media, and browsing, you might not fully leverage its high-end specs. Before purchasing, ask yourself whether you need such a powerful device, or if a less expensive phone could fulfill your needs.

2. Camera Quality and Features

The quad-camera system of the Galaxy S25 Ultra is one of its standout features, with a 108MP primary sensor, 12MP ultra-wide lens, and 10x optical zoom. If you are someone who enjoys photography or creating content, the S25 Ultra is an excellent choice. However, if you don't prioritize camera quality, or if your current smartphone already meets your photography needs, you may not benefit from all the advanced features the S25 Ultra offers.

3. Battery Life and Charging

With a 5,000mAh battery, the S25 Ultra offers a full day's use for most users, but it's essential to consider how much you rely on your phone for various tasks. If you are constantly on the go or use your phone heavily throughout the day, the larger battery and 45W fast charging will likely be a major selling point. Conversely, if your phone use is moderate and you're used to charging it overnight, battery life may not be a significant concern for you.

4. Display Size and Quality

The 6.8-inch Dynamic AMOLED 2X display of the S25 Ultra is one of the best screens available in any smartphone, offering vibrant colors, deep blacks, and excellent clarity. However, its larger size may not appeal to everyone, especially those who prefer more compact phones. Consider whether a larger display will enhance your experience, particularly for watching media or gaming, or if you prefer a smaller device that fits more comfortably in your hand.

5. 5G and Future-Proofing

If you plan to use your phone for several years, it's worth considering future technologies like 5G connectivity. The S25 Ultra supports 5G, ensuring faster speeds and lower latency in areas where 5G networks are available. However, if you live in an area where 5G is still limited or don't foresee needing it in the near future, you may not need to invest in a 5G-enabled device right away.

6. Software and Updates

The Galaxy S25 Ultra runs on Android 15 with One UI 7.1, and Samsung provides extended software support. If you value receiving the latest software updates for security, features, and performance improvements, this is a key consideration. The promise of multiple years of software updates ensures that your phone stays current, but if you're not particular about software upgrades, this might be less of a concern for you.

7. Budget and Value for Money

The Samsung Galaxy S25 Ultra is priced as a flagship phone, and it comes with premium features. However, it's important to evaluate whether you need all the high-end specifications it offers. If you're looking for a phone that gets the basics right at a more affordable price point, you might want to explore other devices in Samsung's lineup or even other manufacturers. Weigh the device's value based on the features that matter most to you versus its cost.

11.2 Ecosystem Compatibility and Accessories

When purchasing the Samsung Galaxy S25 Ultra, considering the ecosystem compatibility and available accessories can significantly enhance your user experience. The integration of your smartphone with other devices, as well as the accessories you choose to complement it, can either streamline your daily life or add extra value to your investment.

1. Samsung Ecosystem Integration

One of the most significant advantages of owning a Samsung smartphone like the S25 Ultra is its integration within the Samsung ecosystem. Samsung offers a wide range of devices and services that work seamlessly together. These include:

Samsung Galaxy Buds: If you're looking for wireless earbuds, the Galaxy Buds pair exceptionally well with the S25 Ultra, offering high-quality sound and excellent integration with the device.

Samsung SmartThings: This allows you to connect and control smart home devices from your phone, such as lights, thermostats, and security cameras. If you already use Samsung or compatible smart home devices, the S25

Ultra will act as a powerful hub for controlling all of them.

Samsung DeX: This feature enables you to turn your S25 Ultra into a desktop-like experience, allowing you to use it with a monitor, keyboard, and mouse for productivity tasks. This makes it an ideal choice for users who want a portable yet powerful solution for working on the go.

Samsung Health: For fitness enthusiasts, the S25 Ultra integrates with Samsung Health, allowing you to track your physical activity, sleep, and other health metrics, offering a complete wellness ecosystem.

If you're already using Samsung devices like a Galaxy Watch or SmartThings-enabled products, the S25 Ultra will offer superior integration, making it easy to manage all your tech from one place.

2. Third-Party Ecosystem Compatibility

While the S25 Ultra is part of the Samsung ecosystem, it's also compatible with third-party products and services. For example, if you prefer to use Google's services, such as Google Assistant, Google Home, or other apps, the phone offers seamless integration with these platforms. Similarly, if you're invested in Amazon Alexa or Apple's services, the S25 Ultra remains compatible with many of these services through apps and integration options.

3. Accessories for Enhancing the Experience

To get the most out of your Samsung Galaxy S25 Ultra, investing in some essential accessories can enhance your overall experience. Here are some accessories to consider:

Protective Case: Given the phone's large size and premium build, investing in a durable case is highly recommended to protect your device from drops, scratches, and wear. Samsung offers a range of cases designed specifically for the S25 Ultra, including Clear View and Leather Wallet cases.

Screen Protector: To prevent scratches and maintain the pristine look of your Dynamic AMOLED 2X display, a screen protector is essential. Options like tempered glass or film protectors can help safeguard the screen.

Wireless Charger: The S25 Ultra supports wireless charging and reverse wireless charging, making it convenient for charging both the phone itself and other devices like earbuds or a smartwatch. Investing in a high-speed wireless charger will allow you to charge your phone without dealing with cables.

Samsung Galaxy Buds Pro: If you're looking for a complete audio experience, Galaxy Buds Pro or other Samsung wireless earphones are a great complement to the S25 Ultra. These earbuds offer excellent sound quality and are optimized for use with Samsung devices.

Samsung DeX Accessories: If you plan on using Samsung DeX to transform your phone into a desktop experience, you may need a compatible monitor, keyboard, and mouse. This setup can improve productivity and make your phone even more versatile.

4. Software Integration and Cloud Services

Another aspect to consider is how the S25 Ultra integrates with cloud services like Google Drive, OneDrive, and Samsung Cloud. With Samsung Cloud, your photos, documents, and app data can be seamlessly synced across your devices, ensuring your content is accessible at all times. For those who already use Google services for file storage and management, the integration with Google Drive ensures compatibility, making it easier to work across multiple platforms.

Chapter 12

FAQs for Prospective Buyers

12.1 Common Questions Answered

1. What is the price of the Samsung Galaxy S25 Ultra?

The price of the Samsung Galaxy S25 Ultra can vary depending on the configuration and storage options. Prices typically start from around $1,399 for the base model with 12GB of RAM and 256GB of internal storage. The price can go higher for models with more RAM and larger storage capacities, so it's important to check for current offers and deals from retailers or Samsung's official website.

2. How is the camera quality on the Samsung Galaxy S25 Ultra?

The S25 Ultra is equipped with a quad-camera system, including a 108MP primary sensor, 12MP ultra-wide lens, 10MP telephoto lens, and a 10MP periscope lens for 10x optical zoom. The camera setup is designed to deliver excellent photos in various lighting conditions, from stunning wide-angle shots to detailed close-ups with incredible zoom. The device also supports 8K video recording and includes advanced AI features for automatic scene optimization, making it ideal for photography enthusiasts and content creators.

3. How long does the battery last on the Galaxy S25 Ultra?

With a 5,000mAh battery, the S25 Ultra can easily last a full day of use with typical activities, such as browsing, media consumption, and light gaming. Battery life will vary depending on usage, with more demanding tasks like gaming or video streaming potentially draining the battery faster. The device supports 45W fast charging, so you can quickly recharge the phone when needed, and it also supports wireless charging for added convenience.

4. Is the Samsung Galaxy S25 Ultra waterproof?

Yes, the Galaxy S25 Ultra has an IP68 rating, meaning it is resistant to dust and can withstand being submerged in water up to 1.5 meters deep for up to 30 minutes. While it is water-resistant, it's still important to avoid exposing the device to extreme conditions, such as hot showers or salty water, which can damage the phone over time.

5. Does the Galaxy S25 Ultra support 5G?

Yes, the Samsung Galaxy S25 Ultra is fully 5G-compatible, offering support for both Sub-6 GHz and mmWave 5G bands, depending on your region and network availability. With 5G, you can expect faster download and upload speeds, improved streaming quality, and low latency for online gaming.

6. Does the S25 Ultra come with expandable storage?

No, the Samsung Galaxy S25 Ultra does not support microSD card expansion. However, it comes with a generous internal storage capacity, starting at 256GB and going up to 1TB, depending on the model. If you require more storage space, consider purchasing a higher-storage model or using cloud storage solutions like Google Drive or Samsung Cloud.

7. What is the display quality like on the Galaxy S25 Ultra?

The S25 Ultra features a 6.8-inch Dynamic AMOLED 2X display, offering vibrant colors, deep blacks, and an immersive viewing experience. With a 120Hz refresh rate, the display is extremely smooth, which is especially noticeable when scrolling through apps, browsing, or gaming. The Quad HD+ resolution ensures sharp visuals, making it a fantastic display for media consumption.

8. Is the Galaxy S25 Ultra compatible with wireless charging?

Yes, the Galaxy S25 Ultra supports 15W wireless charging for fast and efficient charging without the need for cables. The device also supports reverse wireless charging, allowing you to charge other compatible devices, such as wireless earbuds or a smartwatch, by placing them on the back of the phone.

12.2 Troubleshooting Initial Concerns

While the Samsung Galaxy S25 Ultra is a high-end device, like any smartphone, you may encounter occasional issues. Here are some common troubleshooting tips to help resolve initial concerns:

1. The phone is not charging properly.

If your S25 Ultra isn't charging as expected, here are a few things to check:

Check the Charging Cable and Adapter: Ensure that the charging cable and adapter are functioning properly. If you're using a third-party charger, it might not support fast charging, so try using the charger that came with the device.

Clean the Charging Port: Dust or debris in the charging port can interfere with the charging process. Gently clean the port using a soft brush or compressed air.

Restart the Phone: Sometimes, a simple restart can resolve charging issues by clearing any software-related glitches.

Update the Software: Make sure your phone's software is up to date, as updates often include bug fixes that address charging issues.

2. The screen is not responding or freezing.

If your phone's screen becomes unresponsive or freezes, you can try the following:

Force Restart: To restart the phone without using the touchscreen, press and hold the Volume Down and Power buttons simultaneously for about 10 seconds until the device restarts.

Check for App Conflicts: If the issue occurs after installing a particular app, try uninstalling the app to see if that resolves the issue. You can also try booting into Safe Mode to see if any third-party apps are causing the problem.

Clear Cache: Clearing the cache of apps and system data may help resolve unresponsiveness or slow performance. You can do this in the Settings app under Storage and Cache Data.

3. The camera is not focusing properly.

If the camera is having trouble focusing, here are some steps to take:

Clean the Lens: Dirt or smudges on the camera lens can affect focus. Use a soft, clean cloth to gently wipe the lens.

Tap to Focus: If the camera is struggling to focus, tap the area on the screen where you want the camera to focus.

Restart the Camera App: Close and reopen the camera app to refresh the system. If this doesn't help, restart the phone to clear any temporary software issues.

4. Poor battery life.

If you notice that the S25 Ultra isn't lasting as long as expected, try the following:

Check Battery Usage: In the Settings app, go to Battery and Device Care and review which apps are using the most battery. If there are apps consuming too much power, consider limiting their usage or uninstalling them.

Enable Power Saving Mode: You can extend battery life by turning on Power Saving Mode in the Settings. This reduces background processes and dims the screen to conserve power.

Adjust Screen Brightness: Lowering the screen brightness or enabling Adaptive Brightness can reduce battery consumption.

Update Apps: Outdated apps may consume more battery. Make sure all your apps are updated to the latest versions.

5. Wi-Fi or Bluetooth connectivity issues.

If you're having trouble connecting to Wi-Fi or Bluetooth devices:

Restart Your Device: A simple restart can help resolve network or Bluetooth issues.

Forget and Reconnect to Wi-Fi: Go to Settings > Connections > Wi-Fi, select your network, and choose Forget. Then reconnect by selecting the network again and entering the password.

Reset Network Settings: If the issue persists, you can reset network settings by going to Settings > General Management > Reset > Reset Network Settings. This will erase saved Wi-Fi passwords and Bluetooth connections, so be sure to have that information handy.

6. The phone is overheating.

If your S25 Ultra becomes unusually hot during use:

Close Unnecessary Apps: Running multiple apps at once, especially resource-heavy ones, can cause the phone to overheat. Close apps that you're not actively using.

Avoid Direct Sunlight: Keep the phone out of direct sunlight or high temperatures, as this can cause it to overheat.

Allow the Phone to Cool: If the phone feels hot, stop using it for a while and let it cool down. Avoid using it while charging, as this can increase heat.

Chapter 13

Conclusion

13.1 Final Thoughts on the Galaxy S25 Ultra

The Samsung Galaxy S25 Ultra isn't just another smartphone; it represents a leap forward in terms of innovation and technology. One of the standout features is its exceptional display. With a 6.8-inch Dynamic AMOLED 2X screen, the visuals are bright, crisp, and fluid, making it ideal for everything from watching videos and playing games to browsing and multitasking. The Adaptive Refresh Rate further enhances the experience, ensuring smooth scrolling and efficient battery usage.

When it comes to performance, the Snapdragon 8 Gen 4 processor ensures that the phone can handle any task you throw at it. Whether it's gaming, streaming, or multitasking, the phone's hardware is capable of running everything smoothly, with no noticeable lag or slowdowns. The AI-powered features enhance user experience, adapting the device to your habits and optimizing performance for different tasks.

The camera system is one of the most impressive on the market. With a 108MP primary sensor, 10x optical zoom, and 8K video recording, the S25 Ultra is perfect for anyone who loves photography or video creation. Its advanced AI features ensure that your shots are enhanced automatically, making it easier to capture stunning images without needing professional skills. Whether you're taking landscape photos or detailed close-ups, the camera system ensures that every shot is breathtaking.

Battery life on the S25 Ultra is equally impressive, with a 5,000mAh battery capable of lasting a full day under normal usage. When paired with 45W fast charging and wireless charging capabilities, the device is well-equipped to keep up with your busy lifestyle. Additionally, its 5G support means that you can take advantage of faster download speeds and more reliable connectivity, especially in areas with 5G coverage.

The software is another area where the S25 Ultra shines. Running Android 15 with the One UI 7.1 skin, the phone offers a clean, intuitive interface that is easy to navigate and highly customizable. Samsung's commitment to extended software support ensures that users can enjoy updates and new features for years to come.

However, while the S25 Ultra excels in many areas, it's important to note that its premium price tag reflects its high-end status. It is an investment in top-tier technology, and for many, it will be worth every penny, especially for those who need a device that excels in all aspects, from photography and gaming to productivity and connectivity.

13.2 Encouragement to Make an Informed Choice

If you are still on the fence about purchasing the Samsung Galaxy S25 Ultra, it's essential to weigh the pros and cons before making your decision. While this phone offers a multitude of features that appeal to different types of users, it's important to assess whether those features align with your personal needs. If you value a premium display, cutting-edge performance, and state-of-the-art cameras, the S25 Ultra could be an ideal choice. If you find that many of its advanced features are more than what you need, it may be worth considering other options in Samsung's lineup or even from competing brands.

Remember that choosing a smartphone is a personal decision, and there is no one-size-fits-all solution. The S25 Ultra is designed for users who demand nothing less than the best. It offers a blend of powerful hardware, advanced software, and innovative features that set it apart from the competition. However, if your needs are more basic or budget-conscious, there are other options that may better suit your lifestyle.

Before making a purchase, take some time to consider the following:

How often do you use your phone for tasks like gaming, video streaming, or content creation?

Do you require top-tier performance and camera quality, or are you looking for a more budget-friendly device with essential features?

Do you have a preference for Samsung's ecosystem and its accompanying features, such as Samsung DeX or Samsung's SmartThings integration?

These considerations will help you determine whether the S25 Ultra is the right choice for you. Don't rush the decision—take the time to evaluate your needs and explore alternatives that may offer better value for your specific use case.

At the end of the day, the Samsung Galaxy S25 Ultra is more than just a smartphone; it's a powerful tool for anyone looking to stay at the cutting edge of technology. Its superior performance, camera system, and design make it one of the top choices for premium smartphones in 2025, and for the right user, it represents a worthy investment.

In conclusion, make sure that you're making an informed choice. Don't just look at the specs; think about your everyday needs and how a phone like the S25 Ultra can enhance your life. Whether you're upgrading from an older model or switching from a different brand, the Samsung Galaxy S25 Ultra promises to deliver exceptional value and performance, ensuring that it remains a reliable companion for years to come.

www.ingramcontent.com/pod-product-compliance
Lightning Source LLC
La Vergne TN
LVHW022352060326
832902LV00022B/4392